I FEEL TIME'S TIDE

One little drop of color can hit the core

Shahanaz Hoque (Nipu)

 FriesenPress

Suite 300 - 990 Fort St
Victoria, BC, V8V 3K2
Canada

www.friesenpress.com

Copyright © 2017 by Shahanaz Hoque (Nipu)
First Edition — 2017

All rights reserved.

No part of this publication may be reproduced in any form, or by any means, electronic or mechanical, including photocopying, recording, or any information browsing, storage, or retrieval system, without permission in writing from FriesenPress.

ISBN
978-1-4602-8944-0 (Hardcover)
978-1-4602-8945-7 (Paperback)
978-1-4602-8946-4 (eBook)

1. Poetry, Subjects & Themes, Nature

Distributed to the trade by The Ingram Book Company

For my father, Shamsur Rahman

&

My mother, Nazma Rahman

Ms Hoque's poetry collection, *I Feel Time's Tide*, opens with a poem that sets the poet's 'heart's desire' against the backdrop of 'time and tide'. Her collection ends with a plea for 'any soft touch' to recognize the pain of those who fall before fully sharing their gifts, so that they may 'receive their peaceful sleep'.

In *Nothing but Seasonal Plants* Ms Hoque suggests that we humans distract ourselves with 'Discrimination, Pride and Ego' but these are 'little pleasures' and ultimately futile. The forces of decay and death are set vibrantly amidst images of Nature's fullness; 'messy winds tickle the toes of the gentle rivers' (in Season of the Year), 'nature dancing with its own rhythm' (in Tup Tap rainy rhythm). She tells us that she has been prepared to fight for her own sense of rhythm (I was born to fight), 'I was fighting for my rhythm'.

Throughout the collection, Ms Hoque explores the need for balance. New technologies are seen as 'a blessing and a curse'. She wishes, 'take your city and return my forest' so that she can 'love naturally'. Balance and rhythm are essential; 'If my rhythm breaks, my sleeping baby will wake'. In *Orphan Open Concept* the poet cautions, 'the world is not only for fun'. The flower and the bumblebee show us that 'the world is give and take'.

The final two poems of the collection are connected by the theme of waiting; 'I have been waiting a long time for my crystal morning'. There is a poignant lyricism in both poems that can be found elsewhere in the collection *I Feel Time's Tide*.

Cathy Hutcheon

3rd December 2016

A wonderful collection of poems that paints a canvas of life with colors from mind and nature. Some are dark, some are bright, and some are bleak. But the message is clear - a tighter bond between the mind and nature is necessary to learn and apply the lessons of nature to build a better society. The poet makes us to think and look for the alternatives where instead of becoming a lion kingdom, the mankind flourishes to the brightest of its true color of humanity.

- Dr. Sazzadur Reza Chowdury

TABLE OF CONTENTS

I feel time's tide only...	1
Wish to discover the half pie	2
Nothing but seasonal plants	3
"Season of the year" (summer) inspires next year	5
Thirsty hearts are searching the maze	6
New technology, a blessing and a curse	8
Free me from this slavery society	9
New spring, new hope	10
In but out	11
Goes by order and rhythm	12
Lie = fire	13
Orphan open concept	14
Lost myself to be...	15
Everybody depends on others	16
If a world without needs	17
When I am in real love	18
Balancing or not existing	19
If we go with the flow	21
Light and dark value each other	22

Healthy life and save the world	23
Tup Tap rainy rhythm	25
I was born to fight	26
We are living in a civilized lion kingdom	28
Right Power purified our minds like purified water	29
You are my sweet little pie	30
Contaminated in contamination	31
Our stomach is too small to consume the world	33
Population growth, population go	34
Love = power	35
Mind goes like speeding theory	36
Blowing "Fall" closes her door until next call	37
Waiting for my satisfied destiny	39
Don't reinforce me to bloom	40
I see you wide, wide Canada	41
Making new numbers on our willing hands	42
Little dot in the wide world all along	43
Dried flowers have been waiting for peaceful sleep	45

I FEEL TIME'S TIDE ONLY...

Time and tide wait for none
The wind blowing without showing
Time flying without knowing
Orderly, they pass smoothly by

I feel wind only when there is a nice breeze
I feel time only when my heart's desire releases

WISH TO DISCOVER THE HALF PIE

We are in an exciting space

Many ways we grabbed and took advantage of
Many places we did not step in
Many spaces we are imagining

Digging in but still not finding the core
Busting out but not limiting space to explore

Half (½) of life is occupied
Even though an active life
is not always tight

But

Half (½) of life is not nearly
enough to achieve our goals

Whatever is due we do
but wish to have another way to
double our life value

NOTHING BUT SEASONAL PLANTS

Different trees produce
    different flowers' beauty

They all have their own:
charms, scents, qualities, quantities

Beautiful smells less or more, but when
time is over,
    all
        are
            on the floor

They start from the ground and in the end
mix with the soil

    Birth
    Production
    Death

They complete their trail

continued

Only life's bodies are recycling in the ground

their souls are 'known, unknown' in the spiritual round

Humans are no different

only more awake
intelligent

Could we cross the solar system?
    the Galaxy?
even though we have high hopes with
little more abilities?

    Discrimination
    Pride
    Ego

They are little pleasures for us and, in the end,
we are nothing but seasonal plants

"SEASON OF THE YEAR" (SUMMER) INSPIRES NEXT YEAR

Season of the year –

beautiful deep green summer. Wonderful nature finally achieving her vibrant colours. Mother Nature throwing open her doors. Mighty sun always presenting his sunshine. Gentle rivers slowly flowing until messy winds tickle their toes. Naughty birds scratch and chant from branch to branch. Colourful butterflies gift their colours from flower to flower. Noisy insects keep busy with their needs. Active animals dig for whole days, valuing the time until hibernation. Sweet flowers open their beauty, making the surrounding area a dreamy showcase. Nature decorates herself in a new way to celebrate the year so we are all inspired to prepare again

– for the next year.

THIRSTY HEARTS ARE SEARCHING THE MAZE

Flipping the coin, I see
my side is bright
Rounding the ball, I see
a beautiful sphere –
both are light and rounded

Why do clouds shade the brightness?
    Wrong wars
        ash
           a thousand
      years
          but bring quiet darkness

Many guidelines speak their
believing truth,

still,

thirsty hearts are searching their
    real path through

continued

    Thirsty hearts are waiting
    for pure fresh water with which
    to quench the world
    To march together

(adds a lucky charm: to go a thousand years, maybe forever)

NEW TECHNOLOGY, A BLESSING AND A CURSE

New technologies are
boosting up high so we cannot wait
to touch the sky!

On the other hand,
it manipulates our attention
motivating it to fun addiction.

Sometimes it cuts out
all emotional connections,
leaving us only with
careless satisfactions.

"Big obstacle's on the way.
The new, fresh south wind
cannot blow freely away."

Nations are going in a new direction

Sometimes randomly
I wish… take your city and return my forest
so we can free my life with love,
naturally

FREE ME FROM THIS SLAVERY SOCIETY

Self-esteem and self-confidence provide me
    with
        strength

I am my own leader with right and wrong
to consider. No regrets, no blame, if I am not
a minister or a king.

"I am me"
with my own integrity

So I feel rich, strong
    in uneven society
And that releases me from this
    slavery society

NEW SPRING, NEW HOPE

    Slowly river flows
   Nicely breeze blows
     Flowers surrounding areas
       Birds singing
         Animals and insects awakening
      Hints that spring is here
    Spring is here!
After long cold winter
   Washes away old bad nature
    New newborn hopes
      Message a fresh new start
    Wise wisdom wishes
   Lighten our new path

IN BUT OUT

Beautiful world
around me.

>I used to swing with nature
>hugging me, accepting me
>as a part of her team.

Now my inside fire
is a big obstacle
holding my breath in
beautiful fresh air.

>Strong power
>forces me in;
>Massive waves
>push me out

"One little drop of colour
can change the entire
glass of water."

GOES BY ORDER AND RHYTHM

The world goes by with order and
rhythm, the rule for nature.

Thousands of years of civilization
march by one after another.

Nature decorates itself by order –
a butterfly cannot go back as a caterpillar.

If my rhythm breaks, my sleeping
baby will wake.

Rhythm, order, rhythm, order;
they are meant to be together.

LIE = FIRE

Sometimes a lie can be a temporary solution, but in the long term it will break down the main ground.

Sometimes truth is hard to say face to face; it's not easy standing in front of the tiger's face.

But there are many diplomatic ways to get out of it.

>Lie is like fire

>>If you cover one side, fire chunks pop out the other side.

>>Lie is an unusual trick

>>Most of the time it has a certain risk

Sometimes society accepts lying to gain an opportunity – which really confuses the concept "based on our true faith."

ORPHAN OPEN CONCEPT

Open concept
Open concept

Is it a part of the freedom contest?

Some poisonous open concepts
Slither like snakes to poison the child
when they are orphaned

guardian-less

Free winds blow in any direction
Did they turn into the right intersection?

A thousand free minds go as
different fun addictions flow

But the world is not only for fun…

when my original line is not filled up

by "due done"

LOST MYSELF TO BE...

Humans are always motivated by upper branches, looking only for a place in the top alliances.

Big chandelier said to the little candle,
"Don't forget, I am not in your circle."

When beautiful moon came out, chandelier said, "This is my date for the night. My wheels are moving by powerful moonlight!"

Suddenly, chandelier lost itself
as a chandeli–... it's not so easy to become somebody you're not meant to be

(in the end, the chandelier became only a lightless circle)

EVERYBODY DEPENDS ON OTHERS

The flower said to the bumblebee,

> "You definitely depend on me.
> Without my nectar you cannot survive."

Bumblebee replied with a smile,

> "The world is wonderful. Your beauty has
> worth only when we are attracted to you."

The world is give and take.
For less or more
We bond by each other's trade.

IF A WORLD WITHOUT NEEDS

If a human was born without needs
Trade would be flat indeed.

It would be a new planet with new motivation:
    wide
      quiet
        long
we would fill our present needs with
inventions.

Or maybe, we'd only play with fun
mechanisms and fun would be the only
thing in our lives.

Breath would go in a new direction.

Maybe
like a breathless virus without cell connection.

WHEN I AM IN REAL LOVE

When I am in real love
I'm in a dreamy drug
    floating in the air
    my attentions coming into
    one love affair

Rivers always flow
    towards their goal
    desperate until they reach
    their soul

My world is full of wonder
"Love sentence" tying me in thunder

I have lost my power as "me"
My world run by "we"
    sky, rivers, trees,
    celebrating around me

My world is the best because
    you inspired me
    to do my best

BALANCING OR NOT EXISTING

Balance is everywhere
planet, stars
everything orbiting
in their own spaces

If suddenly space becomes
    narrow
    many
    things
    could be
    affected
by the wrong arrow

Balancing will not be effective
unless new forces are defective
Rail lines are parallel
Balancing train runs very well

Too high too low
Too hard to hold the pillar
building and growing
Balancing in life

continued

    Family and carriers go parallel
        side by
        side

    Our world is frightening
    when imbalances
    threaten our existence

IF WE GO WITH THE FLOW

I am flowing and flowing
                with the flow
I am blowing and blowing
                with the blow
Once when I woke up, I found the ocean
                      was so close up

Flowing with the flow is fun
But if not right, could turn,
in future, to a shooting gun

    Do I know my step?

The world is developing on its own speed
but I will pick up, twist up, break up,
depending on what's on the street

I wish to flow
        when my new legacy is
admired for ideal flow
            lighter, brighter
generation after generation
                to glow

LIGHT AND DARK VALUE EACH OTHER

Darkness covers the enchanted world

    Oh, I cannot see
    I need to see
    I live to see

Then radiant moon shows up

    With the glory of light
    Wow, light is bright
    White is wide

If there is no dark, what is light?

HEALTHY LIFE AND SAVE THE WORLD

Knowledge of nutrition
in our brain
helps us take the right train

If our body machine gets damaged
it will produce the wrong image

Healthy body
healthy mind
bring success in our world

Taking care of ourselves will:
make wealthy our family
affect our society
increase world economy

    save it

        from sickness

continued

Deliver a healthy message in early age
a strong pillar
for their next step

Healthy food
healthy lifestyle

The best wish for our future.

TUP TAP RAINY RHYTHM

Tup Tap Tup Tap
The beautiful rainy rhythm
silences my inferior voice
the vigorous rainy melody
draws me in by its incomparable beauty

My voice wants to join it
but my jealousy sprouts
when surrounded by such rainy beauty

I go outside
sky has changed its beauty to dark grey
nature dancing with its own rhythm

My heart becomes anxious
and lost far away

I WAS BORN TO FIGHT

I fought with me
I fought with my family
I fought with my friends and society
I have been fighting with my world to
keep myself as "me"
I fought in my childhood
I fought in my girlhood
I fought in my teenage years
I have been fighting from young to middle
age to become real, somebody
I was fighting for my freedom
I was fighting for my rhythm
I was fighting for my rights
I was fighting for my ties
I have been fighting to keep my rhythm,
so I can swim in my right freedom and save
my "thoughts of property"
I fight mentally
I fight verbally
I even fight physically
I fight intentionally whenever I feel
it's necessary

continued

I have been fighting openly and internally
for a better place to live (according to
my world)
      fairly and in harmony

WE ARE LIVING IN A CIVILIZED LION KINGDOM

My heart was burned but nobody cared
Screaming to the sky, my echo came
    back to my ears
but nobody heard

Trapped
    I was trapped
    I struggled

Everybody watched with wide eyes
because nobody was untied
    Civilized society crossed many layers
We should be in a righteous free sphere
but we live spontaneously in ancient fear

The power-hungry are internally
    unfairly
manipulating the world kingdom

we are living in a civilized
lion kingdom

RIGHT POWER PURIFIED OUR MINDS LIKE PURIFIED WATER

Good (God) believes in a strong power
Pasteurizing the mind like purified water
Some people say we are OK
We know what is due
because it is a civilized society
There is no reason to bind ourselves
into believing boundaries
Society's rules make everything smooth
and put us in the right custody but
Without power can we see?
Can we pass the exam
to run an unselfish business?
No moral lesson, "I am free"
I am only thinking about me
No internal observer, "I am free"
I will only do something
beneficial for me,
even though there is no integrity
No power to lighten my path
Orphan children struggle without guardians
as "unpasteurized milk is quickly
decayed by bacteria"

YOU ARE MY SWEET LITTLE PIE

You are my sweet little pie

Your ongoing electric shocks
    activating our ties

Spending time within your circle,
    I spin all day in a merry-go-round cycle
    Talking, playing, cuddling

Presenting always unexpected
    puzzles

My soul is fresh and round
    when the proper fuel is provided

You are the whole package
    all-rounder
    holding the world bucket

CONTAMINATED IN CONTAMINATION

Contamination in food

> Threatens my health by fresh food,
> eating disorder, so confused!

Contamination on clothing

> What to wear if disease spreads
> everywhere by modern-styled affair?

Contamination in air

> Environment is polluted by
> unbalancing error.
> I cannot breathe in fresh air

Contamination in treatments

> Healthy will be sick by huge favour,
> I have a doctor phobia
> Fear!

continued

Contamination in politics

> Leaders manipulate our needs
> I can't decide on the right lead

Contamination in love

> We are abusing,
> misusing our hearts,
> playing our selves, but of love,
> we cannot trust our real hearts!

Contaminated in contamination

> We cannot die with impure poison.

> Negative plus negative
> becomes positive?

OUR STOMACH IS TOO SMALL TO CONSUME THE WORLD

Our stomach is too small
to consume the world
But our greed will never find
the satisfied wall
It is not easy to fill
life's wishing well
Greed never finding
the bottom of the hole
Pouring but never ending
Exiting mirages
never letting us rest
Little accommodation
but paramount desire
Short lifetime
but too many things to acquire
Whatever one wants does not matter
Whatever is meant to fit
will be there
Greed always wastes our time
and makes our hearts pale,
                discoloured

POPULATION GROWTH, POPULATION GO

Population growth, population go
Manpower boosting all areas to grow
gathering ideas and in turn
building long, strong towers to run
Many thoughts, many strengths
cyclone blowing all over and
producing new inventions

Population could be a big curse

If they are not enlightened by the right path
If there is no harmony the
boat will sink silently
All messy uneven twigs together
cannot build a strong enough boat for survival

Mother of good luck will show
if industries are motivated
by the right and bright glow

LOVE = POWER

Love is the heart of our earth
The biggest power chamber and dreamy drug
All affection lines going through different ends
But all motivated by love sentences
Production cycles pass generation
after generation
The earth accepting biological and spiritual
connections
Other planets are empty, without life
Only earth receives special gifts
Because of love

MIND GOES LIKE SPEEDING THEORY

Minds move like speeding theory
They keep on going with their old faiths,
values and legacies.

Nobody can stop or change their turn
Unless new faiths or values (force) invade
their minds.

Minds flow like rivers
with old legacies newly inspired
Flowing and flowing in certain paths
unless new obstacles move them
off their path.

Sometimes
Spontaneously
I want to lose my mind
but my strong values and faiths

Always
leave my mind
on the line.

BLOWING "FALL" CLOSES HER DOOR UNTIL NEXT CALL

Vibrant colour has gone,
Ripened, colourful beginnings of fall,
    Mother Nature closing her door
    until the next call.

Blowing images take us to a wonderful
Somewhere that proves losing is another
    stage of fun, that
    ending is part of our turn.

Leftovers warn:
Pack up, tidy up
As much as you can.

We become as busy as moles as dynamic
Fall accepts his harvesting job on the nail.
    Now, collections, preservations
    are most on sale.

Suddenly, messy wind shakes tired trees,
Dry red and orange leaves surrounding
    Here, there,
    everywhere free.

continued

Sometimes, gusty wind blows,
whistling day and night
    a lifeless ghost dancing and crying
    in the long, cold, scary night.

Mother Nature is accomplishing her trail,
nearing the end of her cycle as
dull sun shrinks his daylight.
    So we prepare for Cold,
    a long hibernating season's night.

WAITING FOR MY SATISFIED DESTINY

Year
after
  year
    I have
      been
        walking
          in my path;
            I don't know
              where will be
                my final touch;
              Many times
            I was deceived
          by a mirage;
        I could not
      find any-
    thing
      there;
        Where
          can you
            be, my
              final
                destiny?

DON'T REINFORCE ME TO BLOOM

Don't set me up to bloom

Your reinforcements do not inspire me to
groom, though you think you know me well

You set up the path according to you
How will it copy me in there too?

Everybody is individual in their own way
like handprints that do not match

(though you try different ways)

"According to you" can destroy me forever
like random cyclones damaging
innocent plants

You think something should be there
Maybe it is – only, in its own version

Sprouting in its own way
in its own time

I SEE YOU WIDE, WIDE CANADA

I see you wide, wide Canada, wider in
my heart

Your open door introduces me to the world,
the whole world now in my hand, O Canada

I wish: my last breath should be in your arms

The dreams I had, released in my heart's desire
a nice breeze, the flowers blooming one by one
as I first stepped in

Today I see beautiful flowers in combination
and contagious scents around me

Even though I see you from a far, far Canada
always your deep melody hums in my heart

MAKING NEW NUMBERS ON OUR WILLING HANDS

The world is full of varieties
    Some recognized and accepted
    as our daily needs

Many unseen, unknown
    waiting to be scratched
    from the wide ocean

Some foods
    are accepted by tongues
Some melodies
    are accepted as songs

We already found our 0–9
    Now we are making new numbers
    on our willing minds

LITTLE DOT IN THE WIDE WORLD ALL ALONG

I have been waiting a long time
for my crystal morning.

When the fresh spring breeze passed by
with a smile, softly knocking on my door,
my heart became anxious and I had to
rush outside to feel
the whole world blowing around me.

I tried to match its rhythm but I could not,
one piece of the puzzle unknown to me.

So I've being standing
and waiting
like a little dot in the wide world all along.

Spring after summer has come,
flowers opening their showcase again,
but it constantly passes,
the same and the same,
a thousand years passing away

and I am still waiting…

continued

If someone will knock on my door,
I am not sure if
my pale new soul
will welcome him…

like before.

DRIED FLOWERS HAVE BEEN WAITING FOR PEACEFUL SLEEP

Beautiful flowers bloomed
without knowing
in the evening light.

Without gifting their smells,
they dried up early
in the wrong time.

Wide-eyed,
they have been waiting
and waiting
in the branches that
witness their beauty.

If any soft touch feels their pain
it will make them fall in moonlight,
    so they can finally receive
    their peaceful sleep.

AFTERWORD

I was born into a political family in 1972 in Bangladesh. My father was a parliament member and chief whip in Pakistan; he was also the previous Prime Minister's advisor. Before I could be involved in politics, I immigrated to Canada in 1993. Perhaps in the future, I might follow in my father's footsteps and make the world a better place.

I completed my B.Sc. in child development. 5-years music diploma I completed from YWCA. Today, I teach at the Toronto District School Board, where I am also a Bengali interpreter. For the past few years there, I have also worked as a first language assessor and international instructor.

It is my passion to create my own poems, my own music and also sing songs. Life is a constant rush, but whenever I get the chance, and a new message in my heart, I take out a piece of paper and begin. As much as I enjoy creating my own poems and songs, I feel accomplished when I can deliver my message to help the world become a better place.

Sorrow burned me and pushed me to express myself through this book of poems. My mother, Nazma Rahman, wished to visit me in Canada but could not, and fought a long battle with Glioblastoma multiforme (brain cancer) before passing away. After my mother's death, I felt an urge to express myself through the pen and started my first poem for this book. God keep her soul in peace. Thanks, mom, for the gifts you gave me in my life.

I feel a deep connection between me and my father, Shamsur Rahman, who was a potential political leader who did not reach his desired goals in life as he expected. I see him as one of the dried flowers who waits for "peaceful sleep." I dedicate "I feel time's tide" my first book of poetry, to him. God bless him.

(Today, I also remember and thank my elder brother, Mostafizur Rahman (Apu), who helped me at my early turning point, always encouraging me to do my best.

My friend, Sazzadur Reza Chowdury, I would like to give a special thanks to you for your ocean of heart.

Some of my well-wishers directly and indirectly, visibly and invisibly, encouraged me. Thank you so much.

All of my family inspired me in some way but my second son, Tanzim Hoque, always cooperated with me in any situation. Thanks to you all.)

CPSIA information can be obtained
at www.ICGtesting.com
Printed in the USA
LVOW07s0546300617
539867LV00001B/19/P